Summer

For all the lovely children
in this book

The Seasons copyright © Frances Lincoln Limited 1995
Text copyright © Debbie MacKinnon 1995
Illustrations copyright © Anthea Sieveking 1995

Photograph of combine harvester copyright © Malcolm Green,
BMV Picturebank

Frances Lincoln Limited would like to thank the resort of Flaine,
in Haute Savoir, France, for help with the snow photographs.

Publisher's note: no animal has been injured or in any way
harmed during the preparation of this book.

First published in Great Britain in 1995 by
Frances Lincoln Limited, 4 Torriano Mews,
Torriano Avenue, London NW5 2RZ

British Library Cataloguing in Publication Data available on request

ISBN 0-7112-0908-1 hardback
ISBN 0-7112-0909-X paperback

Design and art direction Debbie MacKinnon

Set in Futura Book by Radius

Printed and bound in Italy

1 3 5 7 9 8 6 4 2

THE
Seasons
SPRING • SUMMER • AUTUMN • WINTER

Debbie MacKinnon
Photographs by Anthea Sieveking

FRANCES LINCOLN

Spring

Spring is the time when things start growing, after the cold winter. Georgia can see the buds on the tree, ready to burst into new green leaves in the warm sunshine.

The little buds need plenty of sun and rain to help them grow. It rains so much, Gemma has a big umbrella to keep her dry.

When the rain stops, it's fun to play outside. Sam and Georgia are stirring up the muddy puddles with sticks.

Pretty spring flowers shoot up through the cold ground. These yellow daffodils look bright even on cloudy days.

Sam is smelling the scent of the daffodils.

Ben's daddy has asked him to pick a few bluebells from the garden. If you see wild flowers, it's best to leave them to grow.

Which flowers do you like?

In the spring, lots of baby animals are born.

This little calf is only a few days old. He is still a bit wobbly on his legs.

The mother pig is called a sow. This sow is looking for one of her playful piglets.

How many piglets can you see?
Oink, oink, oink!

Moo, mooo!

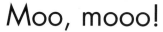

These fluffy little chicks hatched out of their eggs a few days ago. Chicks grow very quickly. Soon they will have grown-up feathers. Cheep, cheep, cheep!

Sabrina is talking to a lamb in the meadow. Baaaa, baaaa!

Summer

Summer days are long and sunny.
It's fun to play outside. There are lots
of minibeasts busy in the garden.
Joshua has found a snail on a leaf.

Lara, Mark and Kelly are having a picnic. It's very warm, so they don't need many clothes. They all need sunhats, though, to keep the hot sun off their heads, and sun cream to protect their skin.

They have juicy summer fruits to eat. What other picnic food do they have?

Kelly is looking for butterflies, but they have all fluttered away. The long grass tickles her arms and legs.

Hot summer days can make you very thirsty. The flowers in the garden need a drink too!

James is drinking a big cup of juice.

Taran is busy watering the plants.

On really hot days it's fun to cool off in the paddling pool.

Jennie is pouring water all over her friends. Splish, splosh!

These children are on holiday at the beach. Nicola and Charlie are digging in the sand. The tide is going out, so the sand is wet and sludgy. Soon it will dry in the hot sun.

Jack is fishing for crabs in the rock pool. What else has he collected in his bucket?

Autumn

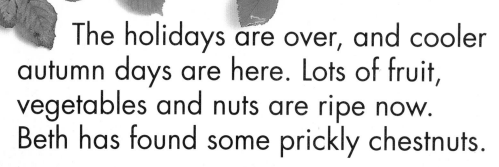

The holidays are over, and cooler autumn days are here. Lots of fruit, vegetables and nuts are ripe now. Beth has found some prickly chestnuts.

Christopher is looking for blackberries in the bushes. He is wearing a jersey his granny knitted, to keep him warm.

This squirrel is gathering nuts to eat in winter. He doesn't need a jersey – he has a thick, warm fur coat!

Autumn is the time to pick ripe apples from the tree. Alex helps to collect some apples that have fallen on the ground.

Farmers cut the wheat that has been growing in the fields all summer.

They use a special machine like this one, called a combine harvester.

Hay and straw are stored in barns. Farm animals eat hay during cold weather. Straw is put down for them to lie on. Jack is gathering some straw for the animals.

Hannah is in the cowshed. The cows will stay here until spring comes.

In autumn, green leaves turn different colours – yellow, brown, orange, red. Ben stands on tiptoe to reach some lovely red leaves.

Strong winds blow the leaves off the trees. Neil is walking through fallen leaves. Rustle, crackle!

How many leaf shapes and colours can you find?

Winter

Chilly winter days are here.
Esme is sitting on a very low branch, with bare twigs all around. Only the evergreen trees, like holly, keep their leaves in winter.

Winter days are very short. It is still dark outside when Jennie wakes up in the morning, and it's dark again by teatime.

She is nice and cosy indoors, but outdoors the weather is getting colder and colder.

What a lot of clothes you need to keep warm…

It takes so long to get dressed in winter!

On cold and frosty winter mornings, the ground outside is very hard. Birds have trouble finding food.

Georgia is putting out bread and nuts on the bird table in her garden.

Now big snowflakes are falling from the sky. Everything turns white. It's the first snowfall of the winter. Brrr, it's cold!

Daniel is so excited – he rushes out to play. Crunch, crunch, crunch. His boots leave footprints in the snow.

Look — here are some more snowy footprints. Can you guess who made these tracks?

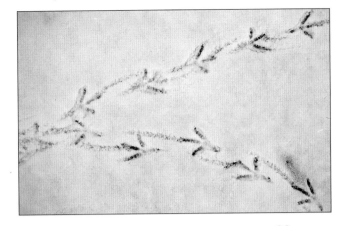

Water can freeze and turn to ice in very cold weather. You can't splash in frozen puddles, because they are stiff and slippery!

The water dripping off Lizzie's fence has frozen, and the drips have turned into icicles. How many icicles can you see?

It's fun to play in the snow. Tom and Sara have made a super snowman.

Joe and Eve are throwing snowballs. Thwack!

Little yellow crocuses peep through the snow. Soon it will be spring again.

Have you ever been on a sledge, like George?

Which season do you like best?

Autumn